maite

WOMEN ON THE EDGE 3

Translated by Margarita Raimundez
Language Consultants: Mila Maren and Tyrone Merriner

RIVERHEAD BOOKS
NEW YORK

THE BERKLEY PUBLISHING GROUP
Published by the Penguin Group
Penguin Group (USA) Inc.
375 Hudson Street, New York, New York 10014, USA
Penguin Group (Canada), 10 Alcorn Avenue, Toronto, Ontario M4V 3B2, Canada
(a division of Pearson Penguin Canada Inc.)
Penguin Books Ltd., 80 Strand, London WC2R 0RL, England
Penguin Group Ireland, 25 St. Stephen's Green, Dublin 2, Ireland (a division of Penguin Books Ltd.)
Penguin Group (Australia), 250 Camberwell Road, Camberwell, Victoria 3124, Australia
(a division of Pearson Australia Group Pty. Ltd.)
Penguin Books India Pvt. Ltd., 11 Community Centre, Panchsheel Park, New Delhi—110 017, India
Penguin Group (NZ), cnr Airborne and Rosedale Roads, Albany, Auckland 1310, New Zealand
(a division of Pearson New Zealand Ltd.)
Penguin Books (South Africa) (Pty.) Ltd., 24 Sturdee Avenue, Rosebank, Johannesburg 2196, South Africa

Penguin Books Ltd., Registered Offices: 80 Strand, London WC2R 0RL, England

WOMEN ON THE EDGE 3

PRINTING HISTORY
Previously published in Spanish by Editorial Atlantida, S.A. (Argentina), 1997
First Riverhead trade paperback edition: January 2005
Riverhead trade paperback ISBN: 1-59448-095-8

This book has been catalogued with the Library of Congress.

Printed in the United States of America

10 9 8 7 6 5 4 3 2 1

To Daniel Kon,
my unchangeable love.

HUSBANDS AND WIVES

if he's late, he wants you to warm up his dinner	if you're late, he wants an explanation	when he showers, you give him dry towels	when you shower, he leaves you a wet floor	if he's ill, you're his nurse	if you've got a fever, you cook for him anyway
if he invites his friends over, you cook up a storm	if you invite your friends over, you know there'll be a storm	if your mother-in-law drops in, you welcome her	if your mother drops in, he takes a nap	if a friend of his comes over, you get dressed up	if a friend of yours comes over, he stays in his pajamas
if he works hard, it's to take care of you	if you work hard, you don't care about him	if he talks about the office, you listen	if you talk about the office, he turns on the tv	if he's not in the mood, he's tired	if you're not in the mood, you're frigid

THE FIRST SIX THINGS WOMEN NOTICE IN A MAN

THOSE MISTAKES WE MAKE WHEN FALLING IN LOVE

SIX INGREDIENTS FOR EVERLASTING LOVE

NASTY THINGS A RESENTFUL EX-WIFE DOES

GOOD GIRLS WITH BAD LUCK

(OR, WHY YOU PAY WHEN MEN LEARN FROM THEIR MISTAKES)

HIS EX NEVER WORKED, YET HE EVEN PAID FOR HER ASTROLOGER

YOU WORK LIKE A DOG, AND HE NEVER SPENDS A DIME ON YOU

HIS EX TREATED HIM LIKE A WORM, BUT HE FOLLOWED HER AROUND LIKE A PUPPY

YOU RESPECT HIM, AND HE KEEPS YOU WAITING HOURS FOR HIS CALL

HIS EX MADE HIM MISERABLE, BUT HE UNDERSTOOD HER

YOU MAKE HIM HAPPY, BUT HE NEVER UNDERSTANDS YOU

WHEN HIS EX ACTED CRAZY, HE WOULD CALM HER DOWN

THE MOMENT YOU FEEL ON THE EDGE, HE HAS YOU COMMITTED

HIS EX WAS DEPENDENT, AND HE TREATED HER LIKE HIS DAUGHTER

YOU ARE INDEPENDENT, AND HE TREATS YOU LIKE HIS MOTHER

HIS EX GAVE NOTHING, SO HE ASKED FOR NOTHING

YOU GIVE HIM EVERYTHING, SO HE ASKS FOR MORE!

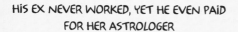

BAD MATCHES

THE SIX WORST THINGS ABOUT DATING
AN UNAVAILABLE MAN

SILLY THINGS THAT MAKE MEN HAPPY

SIX DUMB THINGS THAT ANNOY US ABOUT MEN

HOW BEAUTIFUL IT IS TO WORK WITH YOUR MATE!

CHEERFUL VACATION SHOPPING . . .
AND ITS MISERABLE CONSEQUENCES

ARE MEN GENTLEMEN OR ARE WOMEN INVALIDS?

AN EXERCISE IN WILD FEMINISM FOR REBELS WITHOUT A CAUSE

ARE MEN DEAF?

A DREADFUL FACT: LIVING WITH A MAN MAKES YOU FAT!

IN THE WAR OF THE SEXES, SOME BATTLES ARE LOST BY BOTH SIDES

SOME IRRECONCILABLE DIFFERENCES BETWEEN MEN AND WOMEN AT THE TIME OF A SEXUAL ENCOUNTER

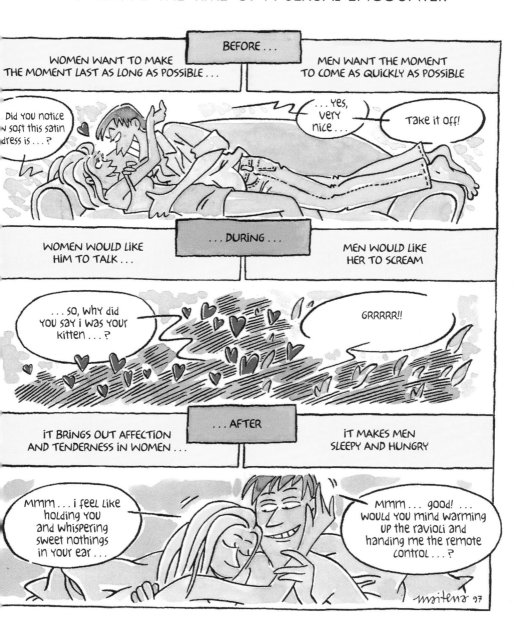

SIX THINGS TO BEAR IN MIND
WHEN MAKING YOUR BRIDAL REGISTRY

WOMEN ARE NEVER SATISFIED

THE TWISTS AND TURNS IN THE LIFE OF A FEMME FATALE

SIX REALLY FRUSTRATING THINGS

TELL ME HOW YOU FEEL, AND I'LL TELL YOU WHERE YOU SHOULD NOT VENTURE

WOMEN AND THEIR CLOSE RELATIONSHIP WITH THE BATHROOM

WHERE DO WOMEN LOOK AT THEMSELVES WHEN THEY'RE NOT AT HOME?

YES BUT . . .

IT'S GORGEOUS!

Yes, but . . . it was incredibly expensive . . . !

IT'S VERY MODERN!

Yes, but . . . LOUSY QUALITY

IT'S SUPER SEXY!

Yes, but . . . terribly uncomfortable

IT'S DELICIOUS!

Yes, but you have no idea how fattening!

IT'S SUCCESSFUL!

Yes, but it stresses me out . . .

SHE'S A SWEETHEART!

Yes, but she makes me feel guilty . . .

HE'S SO MUCH FUN!

Yes, but POOR . . .

HE'S SO ACCOMPLISHED!

Yes, but boring . . .

HE'S SO PERFECT!

Yes, but married!!

WHAT'S THE DIFFERENCE . . .

BETWEEN BEING SKINNY AND LOOKING GOOD?

PUFF...

HREE HOURS A WEEK AT THE GYM

BETWEEN A CLOSE FRIEND AND A BOYFRIEND?

...

ONE NIGHT

BETWEEN EATING HEALTHY FOOD AND DELICIOUS FOOD?

CRUNCH...

EIGHT-HUNDRED CALORIES

BETWEEN BEER AND PEE?

EXCUSE MEEEEE...!

FIVE MINUTES

BETWEEN A BASTARD AND A PSYCHOPATH?

POOR THING...

FOUR SESSIONS WITH THE SHRINK

BETWEEN BEAUTY AND UGLINESS?

ONE FASHION SEASON

BETWEEN BEING LATE AND BEING PREGNANT?

ONE WEEK

BETWEEN SOMETHING PRETTY AND SOMETHING GOOD?

ah.

ONE THOUSAND DOLLARS

BETWEEN AN ENCHANTRESS AND A WITCH?

Ha-ha, very funny.

TWO YEARS OF MARRIAGE

YOU HAVE TO CHOOSE:
EITHER LIFE IS BEAUTIFUL OR YOU ARE BEAUTIFUL

OH, IT'S SO GOOD TO START GOING TO THE GYM!

SEVERAL TRUTHS AS USELESS AS DIETS

ALTERNATIVES TO WAXING

THOSE MOMENTS WHEN LIFE REALLY MAKES A FOOL OF US . . .

FASHION VICTIMS

FASHION FAUX PAS

FASHIONABLE RULES TO FOLLOW . . .
TEMPTATIONS TO AVOID

| DRESS AS IF YOU'RE COMING FROM SOMEWHERE ELSE . . . | . . . from mopping the kitchen floor, maybe? | DRESS UP AS IF YOU WERE SOMEBODY ELSE | Don't i look like J-Lo? — No, more like Jell-O |

| ARRIVE LATE | Oh-boy! Another two hours before i'm actually late . . . ! | ARRIVE TOO PUNCTUALLY | . . . it is the right address . . . |

| IGNORE EVERYBODY, EVEN THE PEOPLE YOU KNOW | Your wife! she didn't say hello! — Relax . . . she ignored me too. | SOCIALIZE FREELY WITH EVERYBODY | Hello! How are you? — Sorry, i don't know you. |

| REFUSE ALL DRINKS AND HORS D'OEUVRES | . . . no, thanks. | GET SMASHED | Don't leave, Ramon . . . ! — Where're the turkey ones yo promised me |

| LEAVE AT THE PEAK OF THE PARTY | But it's great! Why leave now . . . ? — . . . so i'm not around when it dies down- | BE THE LAST TO LEAVE | Left over from last night! |

WOMEN CHANGE, FASHION CHANGES . . .
MEN NEVER CHANGE

SIX AGE-OLD BEACH TRICKS

SIX ATTITUDES TO ADOPT AT THE BEACH TO AVOID FEELING LIKE A DUMPLING

VACATION:
A GREAT TIME TO SHARE WITH OUR KIDS

WE OWE DIAPERS SO MUCH!

THE SIX THINGS A BABY WON'T LET YOU DO

OUR LITTLE TROUBLEMAKER HAS TURNED INTO A RESPONSIBLE ADOLESCENT!

THE UNFORGETTABLE EXPERIENCE OF
LIVING WITH PRE-TEENS

SIX WAYS TO LOOK LIKE A FOSSIL IN FRONT OF YOUR TEENAGED KIDS

TELL ME WHAT SUBJECT YOUR CHILD FAILED, AND I'LL TELL YOU THEIR EXCUSE . . .

SIX MOMENTS WHEN THE MOST IMPORTANT THING ABOUT CHRISTMAS SEEMS TO BE . . . THE CAR!

UNBELIEVABLE THINGS SALESPEOPLE SAY
THAT WE BELIEVE

THE STRANGE HABITS OF REPAIRMEN

THINGS THAT GET LOST IN THE HOUSE

THINGS YOU TYPICALLY FORGET TO REMEMBER

THINGS WE NEVER FOLLOW UP ON

REGRET IS SUCH A SUBLIME EMOTION

RESTAURANTS ARE SEXIST

THE DELIGHTS OF HOME DELIVERY

THE TELEPHONE, A CELLULAR DISEASE

in 1920 women were anxious to fall in love . . .

in 1930 women were anxious to fall in love . . . and obsessed with catching a good husband . . . !

SAY CHEESE STUDIO

in 1940 women were anxious to fall in love, obsessed with catching a good husband . . . and worried about being good mothers . . . !

in 1950 women were anxious to fall in love, obsessed with catching a good husband, worried about being good mothers . . . and restless to study something useful . . . !

in 1970 women were anxious to fall in love, obsessed with catching a good husband, worried about being good mothers, restless to study something useful, desperate to participate in interesting causes . . . and racked with guilt for working . . . !!

in 1960 women were anxious to fall in love, obsessed with catching a good husband, worried about being good mothers, restless to study something useful . . . and desperate to participate in interesting causes!

in 1980 women were anxious to fall in love, obsessed with catching a good husband, worried about being good mothers, restless to study something useful, desperate to participate in interesting causes, racked with guilt for working . . . and stressed out trying to be successful at their profession!!

in 1990 women were anxious to fall in love, obsessed with catching a good husband, worried about being good mothers, restless to study something useful, desperate to participate in interesting causes, racked with guilt for working, stressed out trying to be successful at their profession . . . and desperate to see themselves young, slim and cellulite-free!!

I WAS BORN IN 1962, I THINK. BECAUSE I WAS THE SIXTH OF SEVEN SIBLINGS AND MY MOM HAD LITTLE TIME TO REMEMBER INSIGNIFICANT DETAILS.

COME ON, MARI... LOLI... ANI... CARLI... RAM... PA ...

MAITENA

FROM EARLY CHILDHOOD, I TRIED TO LEAD A NORMAL LIFE.

...BUT I WAS NO GOOD AT SPORTS, I FOUND SCHOOL BORING

AND I WAS TOO MUCH OF A FEMINIST TO BECOME A HOUSEMAKER

SO, I BEGAN DRAWING TO KEEP MYSELF BUSY. AT MY HOUSE, IF YOU DIDN'T KEEP BUSY, THERE WAS ALWAYS A CHORE WAITING FOR YOU.

...SO, THAT'S HOW I DISCOVERED, THAT WHILE I WAS DRAWING, MY THOUGHTS COULD ROAM FREE, WITHOUT ANYONE ATTEMPTING TO EDUCATE ME.

SO MUCH THINKING MADE ME REALIZE THAT, IF EVER I MARRIED, I WOULD NEVER BE AN INDEPENDENT WOMAN.

I WAS ONLY 17 AND WAS ALREADY BEING PUBLISHED IN THOSE WAITING-ROOM MAGAZINES!

STILL I GOT MARRIED, BECAUSE HE UNDERSTOOD MY JOKES.

(UNFORTUNATELY THAT WAS ALL HE UNDERSTOOD)

BY 19, I ALREADY HAD TWO WONDERFUL KIDS, THREE LOUSY JOBS, ALL SORT OF PROBLEMS...

AND GRAY HAIR !

I SEPARATED AT 24

I WAS TOO YOUNG FOR THAT MUCH RESPONSIBILITY

I DECIDED MY LIFE LACKED SOME SEX, DRUGS AND ROCK'N'ROLL

I DON'T REMEMBER MUCH ABOUT THE NEXT FEW YEARS

BUT I USED RED HENNA IN MY HAIR

MY DRAWINGS BEGAN TO SHOW UP IN RACY MAGAZINES IN THE FORM OF EROTIC COMICS. I ALSO ILLUSTRATED CHILDREN'S BOOKS I LIVED IN FEAR OF DELIVERING THE WRONG ENVELOPE.

- BUT THIS IS NOT COLUMBUS ABOUT TO SAIL FROM SPAIN!!

EVENTUALLY, IN 1992, WHEN I WAS JUST READY TO DO SOMETHING ELSE, FED UP BY THE FACT THAT NOBODY SEEMED INTERESTED IN MY WORK, A VERY IMPORTANT MAGAZINE CALLED ME UP ASKING FOR A COMIC STRIP PAGE. IT WAS A SUCCESS. THE ENTIRE EDITING DEPARTMENT WAS IN TEARS...

WOMEN ON THE EDGE!

...SO I BECAME WHAT I'D ALWAYS WANTED TO BE ...

A BLONDE

TIRED OF DESPERATELY LOOKING FOR LOVE, AND ABOUT TO BECOME A LESBIAN, I MET THE MAN OF MY LIFE

ONE HITCH: HE WAS DATING A FRIEND OF MINE

I LOST A FRIEND

_ HANDSOME!
- SENSITIVE!
- INTELLIGENT!
- FUNNY!
- WEALTHY!
- AND MY AGE!

LOVE MADE ME A HAPPY WOMAN. AT 37, TWENTY YEARS AFTER MY FIRST CHILD, I GAVE BIRTH TO MY THIRD, AND THOUGH MY SELF-ESTEEM GREW WITHOUT RESTRAINT AND TODAY MY HUMOR TRAVELS AROUND THE WORLD, THERE'S STILL SOMETHING I FAIL TO UNDERSTAND...

HOW, IN THE END, EVERYTHING TURNED OUT SO WELL

maitena